The British Museum

SO YOU THINK YOU'VE GOT IT BAD?

A KID'S LIFE IN A MEDIEVAL CASTLE

First published 2022 by Nosy Crow Ltd
The Crow's Nest, 14 Baden Place,
Crosby Row, London, SE1 1YW, UK

Nosy Crow Eireann Ltd
44 Orchard Grove, Kenmare,
Co Kerry, V93 FY22, Ireland

www.nosycrow.com

ISBN 978 1 83994 106 1 (HB)
ISBN 978 1 83994 214 3 (PB)

Nosy Crow and associated logos are trademarks
and/or registered trademarks of Nosy Crow Ltd.

Published in collaboration with the British Museum.

Text © Chae Strathie 2022
Illustrations © Marisa Morea 2022

The right of Chae Strathie to be identified as the author and Marisa Morea
to be identified as the illustrator of this work has been asserted.

All rights reserved.

This book is sold subject to the condition that it shall not,
by way of trade or otherwise, be lent, hired out or otherwise circulated in
any form of binding or cover other than that in which it is published.
No part of this publication may be reproduced, stored in a retrieval system,
or transmitted in any form or by any means
(electronic, mechanical, photocopying, recording or otherwise)
without the prior written permission of Nosy Crow Ltd.

A CIP catalogue record for this book is available from the British Library.

Printed in China.
Papers used by Nosy Crow are made from wood
grown in sustainable forests.

1 3 5 7 9 8 6 4 2 (HB)
1 3 5 7 9 8 6 4 2 (PB)

SO YOU THINK YOU'VE GOT IT BAD?

A KID'S LIFE IN A MEDIEVAL CASTLE

CONTENTS

HOME LIFE
Pages 6–11

FAMILY LIFE
Pages 12–15

CLOTHES AND HAIRSTYLES
Pages 16–21

CHORES
Pages 22–25

EDUCATION
Pages 26–31

DIET
Pages 32–37

HEALTH AND MEDICINE
Pages 38–43

BATTLES AND SIEGES
Pages 44–49

KNIGHTS AND TOURNAMENTS
Pages 50–55

FUN AND GAMES
Pages 56–59

STILL THINK YOU'VE GOT IT BAD?
Pages 60–61

GLOSSARY
Pages 62–63

INDEX
Page 64

HOME LIFE

Don't you hate it when you bring a friend home after school and your house smells like TERRIBLE things have happened?

Maybe your dad is cooking one of his cabbage, haddock and onion stews and your mum is trying out an "interesting" new perfume that makes your eyes melt and your hair turn green.

On top of that, your brother has just done the worst bottom burp in the history of bottom burps and your pet cat decided now would be a GREAT time to bring home a stinky dead mouse.

But if you think *YOU'VE GOT IT BAD*, at least your house isn't surrounded by water filled with **HUMAN POO** and animal dung, and the floors aren't covered in lumps of stinky food and dog mess.

If you happened to live in a medieval castle, that's exactly what your poor nose would have had to deal with.

First things first – what do we mean by "medieval"? Also called the Middle Ages, the medieval period lasted for around 1,000 years, from roughly the year 500 to the year 1500, which is just over 500 years ago.

Castles were big news back then. To begin with they were built with wood, and then stone as people worked out how to construct bigger and better buildings. They were homes for a lord and lady – powerful royalty or nobles who were in charge of the land and people in their area, or even across the whole country if they were King or Queen. Their family also lived there, as well as all their servants and staff and other people. But castles were also designed to defend the people and the land around them from **INVADERS**, which is why they were so big and hard to get into.

HOME LIFE

When it came to life in castles, things were pretty basic – particularly in the loo area. Back then, toilet technology wasn't exactly advanced.

There was no flush to carry your, errr, deposits quickly away down pipes into a sewer where you would never have to think about them again (unless you're weirder than we thought). Nope, all poop and pee would simply slip out a hole high up in the castle wall and – **'WHEEEE, PLOP'** – land in the moat that surrounded the castle.

YUCK! What's that dreadful smell?

Edward went for a swim in the moat ... last year!

More on moats later, but basically a moat is a **DEEP DITCH** filled with water that surrounds a castle to help keep invaders out.

Other types of waste would end up in there too, from horse manure to cow dung. So the reek would have been pretty **RIPE** – especially on a hot day.

FANCY THAT!
Castle walls were very thick – up to 2.4 metres – but they weren't solid. Imagine a stone sandwich, with outer and inner walls filled with rubble and mortar. Rather than bare grey stone, some castles were covered in plaster and whitewashed so they were bright and could be seen for miles around. If your job was painting a castle, you'd need a mighty big brush!

Moats weren't the only source of stink when it came to castle life – there was plenty more where that came from!

The main room inside many medieval castles was the Great Hall. It was used for many things, from eating and conducting business to sleeping.

After a big meal, the floor would have had scraps of food and bones littering it, with dogs nibbling on the leftovers and doing their doings. Servants would have scattered dried flowers and leaves to cover up the mess and **MASK THE PONG**.

Just a small warning – **DON'T** chuck your cauliflower cheese on the floor and then tell your parents to let the dog eat it or sprinkle some dandelions on it. Unless you live in a castle 500 years ago, it won't go down well.

I can't WAIT for vacuum cleaners to be invented.

How many times? Wait till the dancing finishes before you go to bed.

The Great Hall could be a very lively place. The main meal was eaten there at 10 or 11 in the morning, with supper in the evening. Later on, tables were moved to allow for dancing and entertainment and straw mattresses were brought out for servants and staff to sleep on.

Imagine sleeping on a mattress made of straw on a floor covered in old food! Itchy **AND** stinky. Not a recipe for a good night's sleep.

At the beginning of the medieval period the hall had a fireplace in the centre of the room, but later the fireplace was in the wall. The lord and lady of the castle would get the seats nearest the fire so they could keep their wealthy bottoms toasty. Less important members of the household had much chillier bottoms.

I think you may have got a little TOO close to the fire, my lord.

FANCY THAT!

Castles could be cold places, especially in winter. Cloth paintings and tapestries were hung on the walls to keep out draughts and there was no glass in the windows, so wooden shutters were used. Next time you pass a radiator in your house, blow it a little kiss and whisper, "Thank you."

As well as the light from the fire, candles would illuminate the rooms of the castle. They were made from animal fat and a castle could get through **HUNDREDS** of them on a winter night.

This candle is making me REALLY hungry.

I fancy a bacon sandwich.

Of course, fire can be risky, so the castle kitchen was often separate from the main building. Accidental fires could easily burn down a castle, which would have been quite inconvenient. The kitchen had massive fireplaces or big ovens, and several animals could be cooked at once.

The kitchen was usually connected to the castle by a passage so that food was kept warm on its way to the hall, as the lord got **REALLY** grouchy if his peacock pie was cold.

HOME LIFE

After supper, when the rest of the household slept on the floor of the Great Hall or in the parts of the castle where they worked, the lord and lady and their children would go to their bedrooms, which were much fancier.

They had thick fur covers, and rather than sleeping on bits of straw they had comfy mattresses stuffed with feathers. Sometimes there was even a little bed on wheels – called a **TRUCKLE** or trundle – under the parents' bed for kids to sleep on. Sounds cool – like a mash-up between a bed and a skateboard!

Wheeeeee!

Where's Gwendoline?

In bed . . . rolling down the hill at high speed again!

One room we haven't mentioned is the bathroom . . . mainly because there wasn't one.

The lord and lady and their children would have enjoyed the luxury of a **LARGE WOODEN TUB**, which was lined with cloth and filled with hot water that had been heated over the fire. They may have used soap made from olive oil and herbs, so you'd end up clean but would smell a bit like a pizza.

Poorer children used soap made from animal fat and ashes, and bathed in barrels filled with water from the castle well or nearby river. Sometimes the water would have been heated, but it was often cold, which would **DEFINITELY** wake you up in the morning.

With that in mind, next time you're considering getting all "talk to the hand" about taking a bath, just remember you could be getting **DUNKED IN A CHILLY BARREL**, so keep quiet and enjoy your lovely warm bubbles.

HOME LIFE

Do you ever wish . . . you had a den that made all your pals literally wet themselves with envy?

If so, you should get familiar with some castle-building techniques from the Middle Ages.

First things first, choose a good site. You want to make sure your den/castle isn't easily attacked by enemies. So you could build it on an outcrop of rock with steep sides, or land that's suitable for a moat.

In medieval times moat-building was a specialised skill – and expensive. When King Edward I added a huge new moat around the Tower of London, it cost more than £4,000 – a fortune at the time (and probably more than you can afford for your den).

It could take **THOUSANDS** of men to build a castle – from stonemasons and carpenters to diggers and blacksmiths, and many other workers besides.

When it came to building, teamwork was the key. For example, masons would build a doorway, carpenters would make the door and blacksmiths would forge the nails, brackets and hinges to hang it.

To finish the castle, it would be given all the best defences, such as an iron portcullis that could be dropped to protect the main doors, **"MURDER HOLES"** so boiling liquid could be poured on the heads of enemies, and slits in the walls so bowmen could fire arrows at attacking soldiers.

Just to be clear – you do **NOT** need murder holes or arrow slits in your den!

FAMILY LIFE

How utterly mind-numbingly annoying is it when your mum or dad tell you to GROW UP, just because you've put strawberry jelly down your brother's trousers or dressed your dog up in your sister's best skirt and top?

So they want you to grow up? What, like squeeze out a big beard, or get a job in an office selling string, or become super-lame and mega-boring like 99% of actual grown-ups? Or what about getting married?

Actually, if you think **YOU'VE GOT IT BAD**, at least you don't **REALLY** have to worry about getting **MARRIED** when you're a kid!

In a medieval castle, your family might have expected you to get married when you were **SUPER YOUNG** – especially if you were the daughter of a noble family. It was the law that girls could marry aged 12 while boys could get married aged 14.

While poorer kids would be far too busy working by that age, wealthy girls who were the heiress to land, a castle or a fortune could be married to the sons of other rich and powerful families at a young age. The marriage would be arranged for them and often the girl and boy wouldn't even know each other beforehand.

If you think that sounds **COMPLICATED** . . . you're right! You'd just have to hope your new husband didn't have breath that smelled of **STINKY SOCKS** and **BLUE CHEESE**, and your new wife didn't snore like an out-of-control steam train.

Mum?

Yes dear?

Can I swap my husband for a mountain bike please?

What family life was like in a medieval castle really depended on how rich your parents were. If your mum and dad were **LOADED** (i.e. were the lord, lady or monarch who owned the castle), life would be pretty sweet compared to the children of the poorest peasants or serfs – which has nothing to do with standing on a board in the sea. Serfs toiled the land outside the castle walls and things could be **VERY** tough for them as they were practically enslaved people and the lord controlled their lives. Peasants had more freedom and a little more money but were still usually very poor.

At the age of seven, wealthy boys might start school or commence training to be a **KNIGHT**, while noble girls would begin to be taught how to sew and possibly to read and write. Peasant children started to take on duties in the castle or on the land.

By the age of 12, rich boys might be learning how to use swords and bows, and girls would be taught how to run the castle household like their mothers. Poorer children would be trained in skills or trades – by their parents where possible – or be put to work in the fields if their parents were serfs. It was backbreaking work, so quit having a whinefest next time you're asked to pick up one pair of your smelly pants when you could be forced to pick **ONE BILLION TURNIPS** in a freezing cold field in the Middle Ages.

I had a dream about turnips last night.

No way! Me too!

How weird. I wonder why?

FANCY THAT!

Henry V had a sword when he was nine, and his son Henry VI had a little suit of armour made for his visit to France in 1430 when he was eight. You could try putting those on your Christmas list, but let's face it, you're not getting a sword.

FAMILY LIFE

Kids' lives could be tough, obviously, but what about even younger children, like ickle-bitty babies? What was family life like for them?

Well, on the day they were born, they'd usually be baptised. That was when they were given a name and when three godparents were chosen to help with its upbringing. While the child's first name was sometimes chosen by parents, it was common for the most senior godparent to give it his or her own name. You just had to hope the head honcho wasn't called **HOOHAHWOOWOOPOOP SMITH**.

> Why couldn't Anne have been the chief godparent?

> Stop complaining, Trumpetina. And tell your brother Bumsqueak it's time for supper.

It also meant more than one child in a family might share the same name. If you think that's weird, you should ask your little brother Derek or your big brother Derek what they think.

Babies were swaddled to keep them warm. That means they were wrapped up tight in a shawl or a blanket, like a little baby burrito. While it was mainly for comfort, some people believed it also helped their legs and arms to grow straight. If you're checking your legs out right now and are totally **FREAKING OUT**, don't worry – those are your knees. They're meant to be bendy.

FAMILY LIFE

In general, the main thing to remember about family life in a medieval castle compared to now is how much **BIGGER** it was. Unless you live with, like, 100 relatives.

You'd basically be living in the same space as **DOZENS OF OTHERS**, depending on the size of the castle. And even if they weren't your actual family, the fact you all stayed in the same building, or at least within the same walls, meant it probably felt like you were part of a massive group.

Just think about the queue for the shower in the morning . . .

How long have you been waiting to use the toilet?

Five-and-a-half hours. OUCH!

Do you ever wish . . . your friends and family were a bit more interesting?

It's not that there's anything terribly wrong with them – but they're just so normal. Well, how do you fancy hanging out with a **TALKING WEREWOLF**, a half-man half-ox, a man with a dog's head or a fish with three gold teeth?

If you lived in a medieval castle you might have heard tales of these weird and creepy creatures. Tales of monsters were a Middle Ages speciality.

Books in medieval times were illustrated with pictures of these strange monsters. Creatures made up of body parts from two or more animals were often painted in the margins and sometimes pictures showed saints or heroes defeating the beasts.

Less **CREEPY** things like mermaids and unicorns were also spoken of in those times, which is nice. Don't worry about the scary monsters, though – all of these things just came from people's imagination. So there's no point checking to see if your pet goldfish has three gold teeth.

CLOTHES AND HAIRSTYLES

Imagine watching your favourite sport and both teams are wearing EXACTLY the same colour strips.

Go on. Imagine it!

It would be **CHAOS!**

The red player passes to the red player who's tackled by the red player who then knocks the ball to the red player who goes past two red players, shoots past the red player and **SCOOOOOORES!**

If it hurts your hairy little noggin-box just imagining it, think yourself lucky. Back in the days of medieval castles, what a person wore could be a matter of **LIFE AND DEATH** – if they were a knight, that is.

Those guys were well into poking each other with "ouch-sticks", or swords and lances as they're also known, and the medieval period was full of knights in armour battling each other to capture castles and generally getting all **FIGHTY** in fields.

Are you on my side or the other side?

If you're planning to poke me with that lance, DEFINITELY your side!

If you lived in a castle, you might have seen your dad or older brother getting into their armour and riding off to war. But in the early days, it was hard to tell one knight from another in the thick of battle. When things get a bit tasty, one guy in a metal suit looks much like another guy in a metal suit.

So to prevent being turned into a dead person by their own pals, which was **REALLY** annoying, knights started putting pictures on their tunics and shields to identify themselves. The designs could commemorate past victories or be symbols of their family history and often featured animals such as eagles, mythical beasts like griffins, flowers such as roses, and bold shapes like chevrons.

They were called **COATS OF ARMS** – which is also another name for an octopus's jacket.

In terms of clothes, this stylish knight gear was pretty important on the staying alive front and brings a whole new meaning to the term "fashion victim".

FANCY THAT!
Before suits of armour came on the scene, knights wore chain mail armour. It was made from as many as 200,000 metal rings woven together into a suit. You could make your own using the ring-pulls from dog food tins (if you have several years on your hands and feel you really need a suit of chain mail armour).

Slightly less important in the death sense was kids' clothing. But it could still be a bit confusing.

Up until the age of around 10, boys and girls wore dresses. Which was handy, as you and your sister or brother could borrow each other's clothes if you were getting fed up with your own.

Muuuum! Henry's wearing my clothes again!

Give it back, Henry – you know you don't suit sunflower yellow.

In the early medieval period, day-to-day clothes were fairly basic. Men often wore long stockings and a wool tunic with a high neck and long sleeves, while women wore a longer tunic with their long hair covered by a hood. Cloaks were popular with both men and women, and richer folk would import silk from the Far East to make fancy gear from.

CLOTHES AND HAIRSTYLES

Please don't meet anyone we know...

By the later Middle Ages, boys wore stockings or tights with a hip-length jacket called a doublet.

Stockings were dyed different colours and were worn with "braies", which were sort of like underpants connected to the stockings to keep them from falling down. And as we all know, there's **NOTHING** more embarrassing than your stockings falling down in public, eh boys?

Girls wore very similar clothes to those their mums would have worn, which you might think is a good thing or a bad thing depending on how your mother dresses. If she's into cool, fashionable gear then that's fine. If she favours **LEOPARD-PRINT TOP HATS** with **NEON PINK WELLIES** and **GOLD LEOTARDS**, then maybe not so much.

In the early 14th century, silk neck scarves called "gorgets" were the in thing among wealthy women. But then they began wearing **UNDERGOWNS** called "kirtles", with a silk or velvet "houppelande" gown over the top, which had a high waist and a long train (a bit at the back which stretched out on the floor) lined with fur. These dresses had long sleeves and high necks, and **FANCY DECORATION** if you could afford it.

The poor were far too busy working hard and surviving to worry about how fashionable they appeared. But for the rich people, such as the lord and lady and their children, looking swanky was a really big deal.

I got this at www.houppelande.com

Well, someone's not doing any hard work today!

Lords and ladies displayed their wealth on themselves and on their children. They'd be dripping with jewellery, silver buckles and **FABULOUS** belt decorations. It was all about showing off – much like today when that rich kid comes to school wearing solid gold shoes and a diamond-encrusted belt.

Has anyone seen Mary?

Help!

FANCY THAT!

In the later Middle Ages, men's shoes with very long curly toes were all the rage. Sometimes they were so long they had to be filled with moss or whalebone and the ends had to be tied to the man's leggings so he wouldn't trip up. If you're looking for a present for your dad's birthday that will make you laugh, you've just found it.

Poorer castle folk would usually make their own clothes. They would spin wool or weave material or buy linen if they could. Do you reckon you could make your own trainers and hoodie? We mean ones you could wear without people gathering round you in a circle to point and take photos because you look so **RIDONKULOUS!**

Speaking of trainers, there's **NOTHING WORSE** than getting them all muddy, is there? In medieval times, if it was wet outside, you could slip shoes called "pattens" over your ordinary leather footwear. They had high wooden soles, which would help keep your feet clean and dry. You could make yourself a pair out of some soup tins glued to a pair of old **FLIP-FLOPS**. Or you could just buy wellies.

CLOTHES AND HAIRSTYLES

19

On the hair front, it was pretty simple if you were a boy and you were poor.

You had a choice between having your head shaved from front to back or having your head shaved from back to front. If you were a total **REBEL** you could get it shaved from side to side. But the crucial word here is "shaved".

If you weren't short of a gold bar or six, you'd let your hair grow long, possibly with a middle parting, which would be much like your dad's hairstyle.

Girls also usually had their hair parted down the middle, with braids on either side. Poorer girls sometimes had plaits pulled up from the base of the neck and tied together on top of their head.

> Should I have plaits, plaits, or how about plaits? No, definitely plaits. Again.

A lot of the time women's hair was hidden under a hat, of course. Sometimes they wore **REALLY** tall pointy hats, while poorer women often wore "wimples", which were large pieces of cloth that covered the head and were wrapped tight under the chin and neck.

One mega-weird bit of headgear was called an escoffion. It was made from material shaped into a huge double-horned creation, with each horn sometimes being nearly **A METRE LONG**! Perfect for flocks of tired pigeons to rest on.

Back to hairstyles, and a really distinctive one you might have seen being worn by a visitor to the castle was that of a monk. They'd have a ring of hair going right round their head, but the top of their noggin would have been shaved **BALD**.

Why not try asking for a monk's hairstyle next time you're at the salon, to give your parents a nice surprise? Just make sure you don't ask for a **MONKEY'S STYLE** by mistake or the barber will cover you in glue, stick **LOADS** of hair all over you and give you a banana.

And there's nothing medieval or castley about that.

To be honest, I think I prefer monkey style to monk style.

CLOTHES AND HAIRSTYLES

Do you ever wish . . . you could get closer to the animals that live in the countryside?

Perhaps you want to cuddle a cow or hug a horse? Well, be careful what you wish for.

In medieval times people in and around castles would have lived in close quarters to animals, which were kept for food, milk and their skins. But that could be dangerous. There are several reports of pigs **EATING** children for example. If that happened, the criminal (i.e. the pig) could even be tried in court and would likely be sentenced to death – although to be fair that's what probably would have happened anyway when it was sausage-making time.

On the plus side, many farm animals were much smaller then, so a full-grown bull was the size of a modern calf, while sheep were only a third of the size of ones you see in fields today, which sounds **SUPER CUTE**. Presumably hens were about the size of a kitten and you'd need a microscope to see a mouse.

Speaking of mice, people in castles didn't tend to keep cats as pets as much as people do today – they'd mainly be there to catch squeaky creatures. Dogs were usually used to hunt with, although people could grow very attached to them. As well as cats and dogs, you might occasionally have come across monkeys, squirrels, parrots and even badgers being kept as pets in a castle.

Anyway, that's enough of that – it's time to take your badger for his daily walk.

CHORES

Psssst! Hey you. Stop doing that and listen up.

We're about to tell you a very important piece of **HIGHLY** classified information.

All mums and dads, grans and grandads, guardians, whatever – basically all grown-ups – go to top secret lessons in How to Really Annoy Kids.

Don't even bother asking them about it – they'll just deny it.
Well, they would, **WOULDN'T THEY?**

Lesson No. 3,527 is Chores. Tidying up, making your bed, emptying wastepaper bins – that kind of stuff. Those little jobs they get you to do at **EXACTLY** the point you're just about to beat the Big Boss on the 593rd level of Space Zombie Weasels 3.

But if you think *YOU'VE GOT IT BAD*, at least your chores don't include pulling buckets full of human **POO** out of pits. If they do you need to ask for a **SERIOUS** raise in your pocket money.

One of the **WORST** chores a kid would have done in a medieval castle was being an assistant to a gong farmer.

A gong farmer had nothing to do with those big metal discs that you bong with a stick. That would be much more pleasant. Nope – a gong farmer was a man who was employed to empty the deep pits that **TOILETS** emptied into (the ones that didn't go straight into the castle moat).

When they were full, the gong farmer would swing into action with his stinky little helpers – usually a boy or two who would lift the buckets he filled with the brown stuff or could squeeze into tight pits if they were **REALLY** lucky.

It's your turn to go into the pit.

Sorry, I'm allergic to tight spaces filled with poo and wee.

FANCY THAT!

One of the smelliest jobs – apart from the gong farmer – was a tanner, who prepared animal skins for use. Once the hair was removed, the tanners would soften the material by pounding dung into the skin. Dog and pigeon poop were commonly used. Put it this way, you wouldn't want to be stuck in a lift with a tanner after a hard shift.

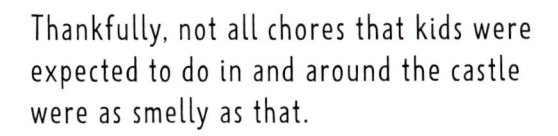

Thankfully, not all chores that kids were expected to do in and around the castle were as smelly as that.

The luckiest children were those who had jobs as servants looking after the lord and lady's apartments. They got nicer food and, rather than sleeping in chilly, uncomfortable parts of the castle, they slept in the **POSH ROOMS** which were warm and comfy.

These boys and girls were often children of wealthy families. They'd be sent away from home and spend years perfecting their good manners and learning how to act like a noble man or woman.

I think you might need a few more lessons.

So it's not good manners to burp the alphabet during dinner, then?

Sounds like it was a bit more detailed than saying "please" and "thank you" and remembering not to blow your nose on the curtains.

There was plenty for kids to do throughout the castle. Unless children were from wealthy families, they wouldn't go to school, so they were put to work instead.

Stable boys mucked out the areas where the horses were kept – and there were **LOTS** of horses creating **LOTS** of muck in those days. Kennel boys helped take care of the hunting dogs. Girls would help with cleaning the castle and mending clothes.

Please let it be a little sparrow for dinner...

Sorry, it's a cow.

In the kitchens, scullions and scullery maids were small boys and girls who did jobs like dishwashing and food preparation. A little lad might be given the task of **TURNING THE SPIT** – the metal pole over the fireplace that had cow, pig, sheep or bird meat skewered on it to cook. The modern equivalent would be spinning the big lump of doner meat in a kebab shop.

If you were a peasant kid you might end up collecting eggs, fetching water, gathering fruit and nuts or herding geese. If you want to see how good you are at that last one, but are short of geese, see if you can encourage a group of pigeons into your kitchen. Your parents will be **WELL** impressed.

As poorer children got older, the chores done by boys and girls would start to differ. Boys would help plant seeds and harvest crops, repair tools and learn how to use a plough. Girls would be taught how to cook and preserve food, as well as milk cows, feed chickens and care for their little brothers and sisters.

Peasant girls might also learn how to make medicines from herbs – which doesn't mean you can rub the oregano from your kitchen cupboard on your pal's skinned knee and pass yourself off as a doctor.

Hi, I seem to have a sword kind of poking right through me.

No problem – just rub this parsley on it.

Wherever their jobs were in the castle, it was a long day for the children who worked. In summer, they could start as early as **5.30AM**! And there was no early finish either – try 7pm on for size.

If that makes you feel lightheaded just thinking about it, perhaps the next task on your list should be "not getting your grumble on about doing a couple of tiny chores". Just a thought.

Do you ever wish . . . you could get a brilliant new game to play because you're SO bored?

How about "Chase the Chicken"? It involves you chasing, you know, a chicken. And that's it.

It might not sound like the kind of thing that's likely to be released as the next big video game, but back in medieval castle days, it was the in thing – at Easter at least.

During holidays and festivals, games like that would have been played, along with lots of other activities – some of which we still do **TODAY**, like painting and rolling Easter eggs.

On saints' days, children dressed as priests or bishops and went round houses asking for money or food. You could always try doing that now, but you'll probably end up being taken home by the police.

At Halloween, kids put on masks and asked for cakes. We're guessing the masks weren't plastic and bought in supermarkets though.

Christmas was a time of sharing. Medieval peeps decorated their castles with mistletoe and ivy, and the big cheeses invited peasants in for a **SLAP-UP MEAL** of breads, soup, meat, wine and ale. And then Grandpa fell asleep in front of the fire and did sprout-flavour bottom burps, which is and always has been the law (only kidding).

Watch out! The chicken's getting away!

EDUCATION

How's your memory? Here's a quick test to find out.

Do you struggle to remember the name of that round green fruit you eat? The one that rhymes with "zapple"?

Do you regularly get lost on the way from your wardrobe to your bed because you've forgotten the way?

What's your name? Did you take longer than 30 seconds to answer that question?

If the answer to all of these questions is "yes" then you officially have a **TERRIBLE** memory. Just to remind you, the thing you are reading just now is called a book.

Don't worry – it's not uncommon to be bad at remembering stuff. But if you think *YOU'VE GOT IT BAD*, at least you don't have to remember loads of Latin words or risk getting hit with a stick.

If you were a kid in a medieval castle, you'd need a **VERY** good memory to do well in school. Actually, that should say, if you were a **RICH** kid. Come to think of it, that should say, if you were a rich **BOY**.

That's because education was definitely **NOT** available to everyone. But more on that in a mo. What were we talking about? Oh yes – remembering things.

Back in the Middle Ages, paper wasn't readily available (at least not until the late medieval period) and the alternative to that, vellum, was made of stretched animal skin and was very expensive. And, frankly, yucky. Imagine writing on a **GOAT'S BOTTOM!**

Stay still – you're making my writing all squiggly!

Excuse me, I'm still wearing that!

That meant that the only way to take notes was to scratch them on a wax-covered board using a stylus, which is a pointy little stick made of wood, metal or bone.

As you probably know from all the wax-covered boards you've written on, keeping notes on them isn't exactly easy. In fact, after being used to write on and the info memorised, the wax would be smoothed over ready for reuse.

That meant kids had no option but to cram a **HUGE** amount of learning into their craniums so they could spout it out later for exams. Again, these tests weren't written on paper, they were done verbally.

Just one more teeny-tiny fact?

Please no! My head will literally BURST!

Luckily all they had to learn was the names of the top five vegetables, a couple of nursery rhymes and the answer to the sum, what is 4 + 2? So it was **SUPER** easy!

If only that were true. But of course it's complete pufflewaffle (yes, we did just make that word up).

EDUCATION

A big part of education back then involved learning lots of Latin grammar.

Latin is the language of the ancient Romans and was used as the common language for educated types throughout Europe during the medieval period.

As well as Latin, subjects could include rhetoric (the art of persuasive speaking), logic (the study of proof and evidence), arithmetic, geometry, astronomy and music.

Using rhetoric, I will now persuade you to give me all your sweets.

Using logic, I will prove to you that you're a nincompoop if you think that's happening.

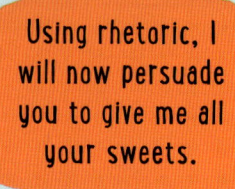

FANCY THAT!

Children liked tongue-twisters back then. Here's one found in a manuscript from Lincoln, in England. Try getting your tongue round it:
"Thre gray gredy geys [Three grey greedy geese]
Fliyng over three greyn gresy furs; [Flying over three green grassy furrows]
The geys was gray and gredy; [The geese were grey and greedy]
The furs was greyn and gresy. [The furrows were green and grassy]."

So those rich boys had to squeeze **A LOT** into the space between their ears.

Yes – rich boys. Remember? Because if you were a girl or you were poor, your chances of getting as good an education as a boy were slim. And if you were a poor girl your chances were **ABSOLUTELY ZERO**. Nothing. Nada. Diddly squat.

EDUCATION

Needlework, singing, playing a musical instrument and even archery were taught to some girls, but not much in terms of schoolwork.

While the daughters of the lord and lady of the castle might be educated a bit, and if a girl became a **NUN** she could get a good education, very few peasant girls would be taught to read or write. In those times it was believed that a woman's role in life was only to look after a household and a family, not to learn things.

Let's hear a big **"WHOOP!"** that this belief is far less common these days.

If you don't let us go to school, we'll teach YOU a lesson!

What does one sword plus one bottom equal?

What?

Correct!

OUCH!

For poor kids – both girls and boys – education was simply too expensive.

It cost money to have a teacher or a tutor, and peasants had very, very little of that. Poor kids also had no time to be educated – they were expected to work from a young age, and were almost considered adults by the age of 11 or 12.

It's hard to go to school when you spend all day toiling in the fields doing backbreaking farm work to feed the people in the castle. Remember that next time you have a **TANTRUM** about doing PE.

Speaking of tantrums, if you were badly behaved in class in the Middle Ages, you wouldn't be given a talking to or get a stern glare from the teacher. **OOOOOOH NO**.

Back then it would be a much more painful punishment – a beating by stick or by hand usually.

As **HORRIBLE** as it sounds, that was very common – in fact it was encouraged, as it was thought that being whacked was actually good for the child. Medieval writers wrote that pain helped students memorise their mistakes, that fear was "the origin of wisdom" and that beating could "instil morality into the students".

One also advises that "beating should always happen before an audience", which sounds like the worst TV talent show **EVER!**

You're DEFINITELY not going through to the final!

I thought I was great!

I didn't!

All in all, if you're given a choice between school now or school then, always choose now.

And don't forget it.

Do you ever wish . . . that your parents weren't so harsh when it comes to punishing you for being naughty?

OK, so you destroyed the entire school because of **THAT** science experiment that went slightly wrong, but did they really have to ground you for a whole weekend?

Think yourself lucky, though. If you were caught doing bad things in a medieval castle you might have ended up in the dungeon . . . or much worse.

Although many castle rooms that were used to hold wrongdoers were usually just cellars rather than actual dungeons, some castles had really unpleasant rooms that were built just for that purpose. St Andrews Castle in Scotland had a notorious "bottle dungeon", which was a dark, damp and **AIRLESS** hole cut out of solid rock below one of the towers.

Of course, for criminals or people that the king or lord **REALLY** didn't like, punishments could be gruesome. If criminals or enemies were sentenced to be executed, their heads could end up on poles on castle walls or city gates as a warning to others. That sounds quite a bit worse than being grounded.

EDUCATION

DIET

Is there ANYTHING worse than being served dinner when visiting a relative and it's something you hate so much it feels like your stomach is trying to escape out of your bottom and run away?

Even worse – you've been given an EXTRA-LARGE portion. And by the looks you're getting from your mum and dad, you'd better eat it all or there'll be BIG trouble for little you.

The thing is, it's probably just sprouts or broccoli or steak and kidney pie or something.

But if you think *YOU'VE* GOT IT BAD, if you were sitting down to a banquet in a medieval castle you might have been dished up an ACTUAL WHALE!

Imagine trying to squeeze that into your poor belly.

A whale might not have been on the menu very much, but DOLPHINS and PORPOISES were probably seen more often – along with a whole lot of very weird and sometimes very wonderful dishes.

Do you want any more dolphin?

No thanks – I'm FIN-ished! Get it?

DIET

The rich members of the household – i.e. the lord and lady and their kids, as well as important guests – would at times have dined on some pretty unusual nosh.

You might have nibbled on **PEACOCK** or chomped a **SEAL**. Or how about some tasty **SWAN**? **ROAST HERON** and **PIG'S HEAD**? Perhaps a little bite of **OTTER**?

Feeling sick yet?

No? Well how about a pie filled with **LIVE ANIMALS**, like frogs or blackbirds? That's what the lord might have put on to impress guests. A lovely **FROG PIE** – where the filling hops off your plate before you can eat it (which is probably a good thing for all concerned – especially the frogs).

How do you feel about being put inside a pie?

Hopping mad!

FANCY THAT!

When a banquet took place, some animals that had been cooked were decorated so they looked like they were still alive. If it was a bird, the feathers would be replaced and it would be coloured with fruit or vegetable juices. Hopefully your parents don't get any ideas next time you have chicken nuggets for tea.

What about pudding? Are you a fan of jelly and custard? Well, in the castle they were dyed with bright colourings that the cooks got from natural sources. If you wanted red, you'd use sandalwood or saffron for yellow. Fancy a nice black custard? You'd use **BOILED BLOOD**! Standard yellow custard is fine for us. Honestly. Thanks.

Of course, banquets weren't filled entirely with stomach-churning oddities. There were simpler foods in there too – and some amazing ones.

The most impressive things on the banquet table were incredible **SUGAR SCULPTURES** known as "subtleties". These eye-catching creations were of castles, ships, famous philosophers or scenes from stories. Not something you're likely to see down at your local burger joint.

How many sugars do you take in your tea?

FANCY THAT!
In castle kitchens, the animal fat from cooking was used over and over. The kitchen would be locked overnight to stop servants stealing fat for a little treat. You can see how bad things were if greasy old fat was considered a treat.

Err, how about NONE – until I win the lottery or something!

Wealthy people would enjoy freshly killed meat and fish caught from local rivers. They'd also have fresh fruit and dishes flavoured with spices like ginger, nutmeg, cardamom and pepper.

Spices like these, as well as salt and sugar, were very expensive, so if you were a poorer kid in the castle, your meals would be **MUCH** plainer. You'd eat stuff like bread, pottage (thick vegetable soup), bacon, milk and cheese.

Not quite as tasty, but probably better than chewing on a dolphin or **CHASING** a frog with a fork.

Actually, that wouldn't have happened, because forks weren't around until later. People would tend to eat with a knife, a spoon or their fingers.

And when it came to plates, there was an unusual alternative. Called "trenchers", they were thick slices of stale bread that food was served on. Afterwards they were sometimes handed out to the poor to eat, which certainly saved on washing-up.

This trencher tastes even worse than usual!

Whoops! That's an actual plate.

Do you ever wish... you could go on a TV talent show and really blow them away with something they'd never seen or heard before?

Well you need to get yourself a lizard! We're not suggesting you blow into a chameleon to make it parp – a "lizard" was an S-shaped wooden instrument from medieval times. If you were enjoying some musical entertainment during a banquet, you might have heard one of these tootling away.

If you can't get your hands on a lizard, try grabbing a "crumhorn" or a "hurdy-gurdy" – that should impress the judges. They were also instruments you might have heard back then.

A crumhorn had **NOTHING** to do with little bits of cake – it was a curved woodwind instrument that looked a bit like an upside-down walking stick.

A hurdy-gurdy meanwhile looked like a weird guitar, except you turned a handle that rubbed against the strings to make a droning sound. A bit like the noise your dad makes when he's talking about something **INCREDIBLY** boring.

"Lutes" were popular too – they looked kind of like a pear-shaped guitar with a bent neck. You won't see many pop bands playing them these days.

There were plenty of instruments around then that are still played today, though, from drums of various kinds, to harps, flutes and bagpipes. Time to get that medieval supergroup together for Castle's Got Talent!

DIET

Of course, there were no fridges back then, due to a distinct lack of plug sockets.

Instead meat and fish were salted to preserve them, while sauces could be used to mask the **YUCKY TASTE** of meat that was past its best.

And what would you drink to wash down your meal if you were a kid back then? Well, you'd certainly drink water, but what else? Orange squash? Banana milkshake? A zingy isotonic sports drink?

Naaah. You'd sip a nice low-alcohol beer called small beer.

That's right – even the **KIDS** drank beer! And before you ask, no, you're not having any for supper.

Somebody had to make all this stuff of course, and the castle kitchens – which were hot, **NOISY** places with huge fireplaces and ovens – would have been staffed with cooks, "sauce-makers", and butlers and their child helpers. "Pantlers" were in charge of the pantry, not making pies filled with pants – although given some of the other dishes on offer that wouldn't have been too surprising.

FANCY THAT!

Some castles had huge numbers of staff working in them. At Goodrich Castle in England, the Lady who owned it, Countess Joan de Valence, had nearly 100 servants. And there's you having to make do with zero servants. It's just not fair!

Another food-related job that someone in your family might have done was being a **"TASTER"**, which involved trying the food of a royal or noble to make sure it wasn't **POISONED** or off. If it was and you discovered it, you were given a pat on the back and a big pay rise. Unfortunately, you were also dead.

Congratulations on spotting that the king's food was poisoned!

And commiserations on being dead.

...

When it came to manners at the table, there were books to make sure you knew what not to do.

One 15th century book had the following advice:

Do not spit upon the table.
Do not pick your teeth at the table with a knife, straw or stick.
Do not burp near anyone's face if you have bad breath.

Another guide advised diners **NOT** to do bottom burps, pick their noses or scratch flea bites at the table.

BUUUUUUUUURRRRRRP!

You still haven't read that book I gave you, have you?

But hey – this ain't the medieval period . . . so you can do **ALL** of those things!

Happy burping!

HEALTH AND MEDICINE

Hands up if you get really excited about going to the dentist because you love it SO MUCH and it's even better than getting a new bike or winning a top-of-the-range computer.

Let's have a quick count of hands. That's one, two, three, four . . . oh, hang on. That's **NONE!** Zero hands. A complete absence of handy things.

That's not surprising. While it might be necessary to go to the dentist and you should **ALWAYS** do it when you need to and dentists are **GREAT PEOPLE** with lovely teeth, no one **LOVES** going to get their teeth drilled, prodded, scraped or pulled out.

But if you think *YOU'VE GOT IT BAD*, at least you get to go to an actual dentist in a surgery with a proper chair and equipment and one of those big lights and pink stuff to slosh round your mouth afterwards.

In medieval times, if you wanted dental work done, you'd probably end up in a booth at a **FAIR** or market! Imagine going to your local fair and instead of going on the dodgems, you get a tooth yanked out! Not as much fun, eh?

> You can get candyfloss AFTER you've had those three teeth pulled out.

> Awww, Muuuum!

If the folk at the fair didn't do it, your friendly neighbourhood **BARBER** would. That's right! The person who cut your hair would also remove your molars. Just nip down to your local hair salon and ask for a quick trim and a couple of false teeth please!

But hey, at least they had anaesthetics to stop the pain just like they do today. Wait. What's that? Oh yeah – they **DIDN'T!** The rotten old teeth were just yanked out with a pair of pliers and **NO** pain relief. Probably stung a little.

FANCY THAT!
Rich kids had toothpaste made from flour, honey and mint mixed with a metal called alum. They didn't have toothbrushes though, so they'd just have to use their finger or a twig. Poor kids used a cloth to wipe their teeth. As long as they didn't get mixed up with the cloth for cleaning the loo. Yeuch!

This finger is so handy!

HEALTH AND MEDICINE

If you think dentists were bad, you should have seen the doctors.

Or rather, you SHOULDN'T have seen the doctors if you wanted to avoid pain or DEATH, which you should definitely steer clear of if you want to enjoy life.

It was definitely a bad idea to get ill or injured in a medieval castle. The average life expectancy in the middle of the Middle Ages was only around **30-35**, and 1 in 5 children died before their first birthday.

Docs back then just loved **EMPTYING BLOOD** out of their patients. They reckoned it was the cure for almost any illness.

Sometimes they would cut open a vein and let the blood drain out into a **BLOODLETTING CUP**. The phases of the moon, the tides and the season would help them decide which vein to cut, but whatever the choice the end result could easily be a dead patient.

Just sit down there while I fetch my very sharp knife.

Are you sure that's the best cure for a sore throat?

Less dangerous, but more "YEUCH", was the use of leeches. If you don't know what a leech is, imagine a slippery green/black slug with a mouth filled with sharp teeth that it uses to bite you and **SUCK YOUR BLOOD** until it's completely full (and you are less so).

40

Docs would stick these onto their patients and let them gobble away until the patient was better, which was quite unlikely. If anything, it probably made them weaker.

I think this one has been eating garlic.

Yuck! He tastes awful!

I'll have yours – I love garlic!

Amazingly, leeches are still used in medicine today! But docs only pop them onto certain patients to improve blood-flow to particular areas of the body rather than believing they cure everything.

Aside from all this blood business, many treatments were a mixture of herbal remedies and supernatural ideas. Many people believed illness was caused by witchcraft, demons, curses, bad smells and the will of God. Because of this, people would do things like smell strong flowers, use charms to ward off evil and even have **HOLES DRILLED** into their skull!

Do you ever wish . . . you were magic?

It would come in really handy. You could make jam doughnuts appear in a puff of smoke or turn your teacher into a pink baboon. Well, in medieval times, magic and charms were everywhere – and some of it was pretty weird.

Sealskin was used as a charm to repel lightning, while a hare's foot tied to the left arm would protect you from danger. We strongly urge you **NOT** to try these out. It won't be good for you or for the seals and hares.

Another animal-related belief was that dabbing yourself with the blood of a lion would keep you safe from all other beasts. Great – no more wasp stings! Only problem was you had to get a blood sample from a lion. Wasp sting or lion bite – you decide.

Herbs were also said to have magical properties – and we're not talking about a bag of basil from your local supermarket. For instance, sprigs of rosemary at your door were thought to ward off venomous snakes, while five nettle leaves held in the hand would save you from fear (presumably not the fear of getting nasty nettle stings, though).

One of the **WEIRDEST** magical beliefs was that sage allowed to decay while surrounded by dung would create a bird with a serpent's tail. Anyone who touched it would go out of their mind for 15 days. Don't you just **HATE** it when that happens? Annoying herb-poop bird!

HEALTH AND MEDICINE

If you did catch a disease, you'd be lucky if you got better.

The **PLAGUE** (or Black Death as it became known) was a particularly nasty one – you'd definitely get a day off school if you caught it. You'd get red spots on your skin, sore **BLACK BULGES** under your arms, fever, vomiting, headaches and you'd start coughing up blood!

Plague, I see. Well, you'd better sit out games, I suppose.

Thanks, sir.

You could also catch the likes of **SMALLPOX**, which could result in you being less alive than you were before you caught it.

Even if you didn't die from a disease, life could be tough. If you had **LEPROSY**, you'd be treated like an outcast and made to ring a bell to warn people you were coming. People would throw food for lepers, but they wouldn't come near them for fear of infection.

Not exactly a barrel of laughs to be ill in a medieval castle then.

FANCY THAT!

Medieval docs didn't know much about how the plague was spread from one person to another. One medic at the time is said to have claimed, "instantaneous death occurs when the aerial spirit escaping from the eyes of the sick man strikes the healthy person standing near and looking at the sick". Unfortunately, keeping your eyes shut did not stop you from catching the plague.

But not all medieval medicine was bad.

Some medieval treatments may have been successful, from **HERBAL REMEDIES** used by wise women to ways of mending broken bones.

With the castle's knights and soldiers fighting battles, or even just training for war, there were plenty of opportunities to learn techniques like setting broken bones in plaster and sealing wounds using **EGG WHITES**. Old wine would be used to stop wounds getting infected and certain plants could send people to sleep when operations were taking place.

This knight has terrible wounds!

Quick! Fetch the eggs!

Archaeologists have discovered evidence of broken bones healing perfectly and skeletons of people who survived nasty sword wounds, so at least some docs (and barbers) knew what they were doing.

Still, if you ever travel back in time to a medieval castle and some guy comes at you with a **HUNGRY LEECH**, do yourself a favour and get back in your time machine pronto.

HEALTH AND MEDICINE

BATTLES AND SIEGES

So you've just done something REALLY naughty, like robbed a bank, taken a busy cruise ship for a sail without asking or been a bit cheeky to your gran.

You run up to your room and barricade yourself in. There's no way anyone can get you out.

But, after a while, you start to get hungry. You eat that half-flapjack from under the bed, nibble the mouldy orange from the windowsill (including dead flies) and drink something that may have once been milk but is now green and cheesy.

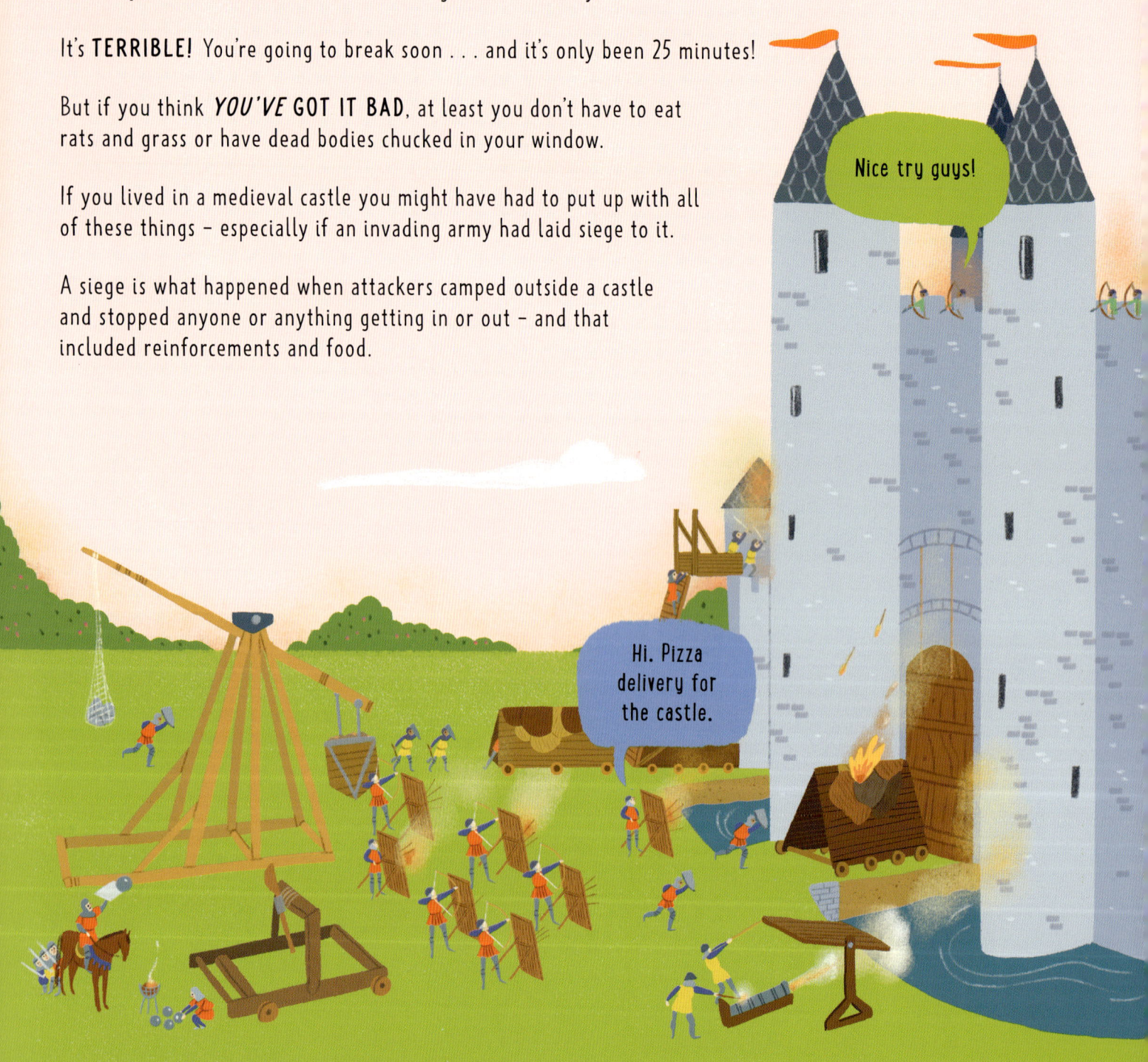

It's **TERRIBLE!** You're going to break soon . . . and it's only been 25 minutes!

But if you think *YOU'VE* **GOT IT BAD**, at least you don't have to eat rats and grass or have dead bodies chucked in your window.

If you lived in a medieval castle you might have had to put up with all of these things – especially if an invading army had laid siege to it.

A siege is what happened when attackers camped outside a castle and stopped anyone or anything getting in or out – and that included reinforcements and food.

Attackers would try to break into the castle and take it by force, but if that didn't work, they'd simply wait until supplies ran out and the people inside starved to death or surrendered. And that's where having a lovely ratburger with a side of grass came in.

FANCY THAT!

Because sieges could last a long time, many castle builders tried to prepare by building secret tunnels that led under the castle walls so supplies could be sneaked in without the enemy knowing. It was really handy if the other end of the tunnel came out in a supermarket car park.

There would be supplies kept inside the castle just in case of sieges, but they wouldn't last forever. Sieges could last months or even **YEARS** and eventually the grub ran out, which was when the defenders had to take **DRASTIC ACTION**. Horses would end up on the menu, followed by cats and dogs (sorry pets) and then rats, creepy-crawlies and grass.

Why is that guy looking at us and licking his lips?

I'm not sure, but something tells me it's time to find that secret tunnel.

Makes you think twice about grumbling about Dad's latest dinner concoction, doesn't it? Unless he's serving you **SPIDERS ON TOAST** followed by next door's **POODLE**.

To make things even worse for the poor peeps inside the castle, attackers would catapult all sorts over the walls. We're talking **SEWAGE**, **DEAD BODIES** or even **SEVERED HEADS!** The aim was to spread disease and make people feel **REALLY** grossed out, which worked on both counts, especially if you were allergic to severed heads.

Who are you?

I'm no body.

I hope your jokes were funnier when you were alive.

BATTLES AND SIEGES

Of course, it wasn't all about sitting around waiting or throwing body parts and poo around the place. The attackers also did what their name suggests – attack!

Kids were sent to the safest places of the castle along with the women when an attack took place, but it must have been properly, pant-wettingly **TERRIFYING**.

Attackers would use massive ladders or wooden "siege towers" packed with men to try to get over the castle walls, although defenders would shoot at them with arrows, push the ladders off with long poles or **THROW ROCKS** down on them, so it was no walk in the park. If it sounds like it was, you're walking in the wrong kind of park.

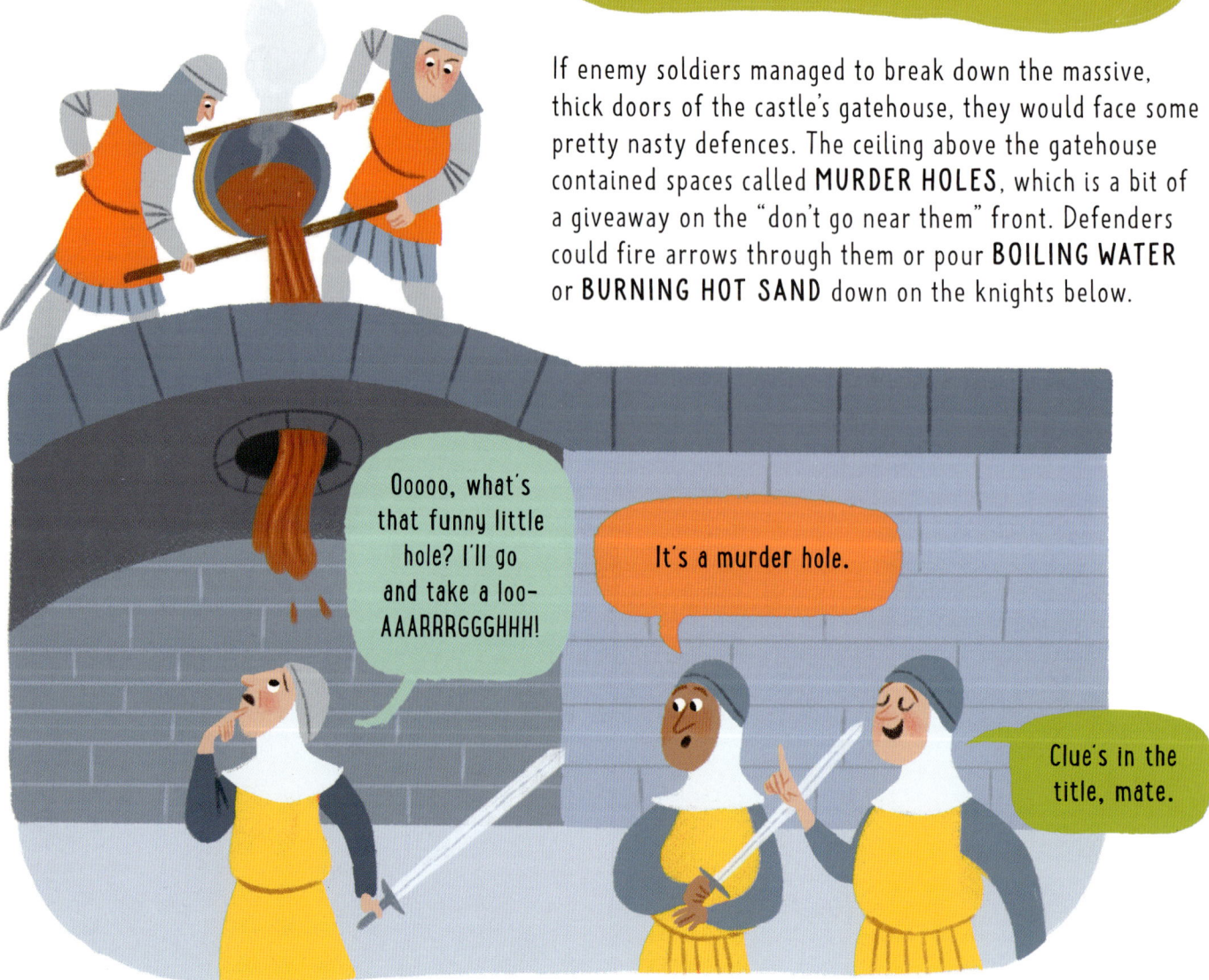

If enemy soldiers managed to break down the massive, thick doors of the castle's gatehouse, they would face some pretty nasty defences. The ceiling above the gatehouse contained spaces called **MURDER HOLES**, which is a bit of a giveaway on the "don't go near them" front. Defenders could fire arrows through them or pour **BOILING WATER** or **BURNING HOT SAND** down on the knights below.

Ooooo, what's that funny little hole? I'll go and take a loo- AAARRRGGGHHH!

It's a murder hole.

Clue's in the title, mate.

It's often said that they used boiling oil or fat, but that was too expensive. Why waste good boiling fat when you could use cheap hot sand and save the boiling fat for all those things you use boiling fat for? Like, errrr . . . we'll get back to you on that.

If the straightforward route failed, something bigger was required.

Men in the invading army called "sappers" would dig tunnels and when they were under the castle walls, they'd set fire to the wooden supports holding up the roof, and **CRASH!** The tunnel, and the walls above, would come tumbling down.

Catapults and other huge weapons were also used to hurl boulders at the walls to try to destroy them. Sometimes catapults went wrong, which could have **GRIM** results. Knights and men could be crushed by boulders from their own weapons if they broke and only threw their projectiles a short distance. A suit of armour wasn't much protection from a rock the size of a **CAR**!

BATTLES AND SIEGES

If none of that worked, sometimes enemy armies used dirty tricks to try to sneak in.

For example, they could pretend to be merchants coming with supplies and then, when the defenders opened the gates, the attackers would pour in and poke them with sharp things. Surprise!

You'd have to be a pretty dim-witted defender to fall for **THAT** one! Especially in the middle of a siege.

Let me in. Here's my merchant ID.

It's written in crayon and you have loads of soldiers hiding behind you. Goodbye.

Finally, there was one potential way into the castle for any particularly **DETERMINED** attacker.

The castle toilets often emptied straight down a chute, out of a hole and into the moat. If a soldier could get into the hole and slither up the smelly chute and emerge from the toilet, he could try to sneak down and let his pals in to attack the castle.

Of course, if someone was using the toilet at the time, he'd end up with egg on his face. Or **MUCH** worse.

FANCY THAT!
Edward I had a giant trebuchet – sort of like a slingshot – named Warwolf. That was the third name he tried, after Battlehamster and Fightkitten, which didn't really work. Apparently his enemies surrendered as soon as they saw it, which isn't surprising really, as it's a bit scarier than a water pistol or a peashooter.

BATTLES AND SIEGES

Do you ever wish . . .

you could give in to your mischievous streak while at the beach and suddenly jump all over your sister or brother's magnificent sandcastle that they've spent literally 10 HOURS building?

Never mind jumping – that's SO low-key. What you need are some medieval siege weapons. These giant objects were built to destroy thick castle walls and doors, allowing attackers to capture the building and end the siege.

One of the BIGGEST weapons was called the "trebuchet". It was an enormous slingshot – so big that you'd probably need at least two of your pals to help you work it. Actually, it took a WHOPPING 60 men to load and fire it, allowing it to hurl huge boulders and barrels of flaming tar the distance of three football pitches.

A smaller catapult-style device was the "mangonel", which fired big rocks over 180 METRES, smashing stone and wood to pieces. The "battering ram" wasn't an angry sheep, it was an iron-tipped tree trunk on wheels that was crashed against walls and doors to break them down.

The coolest-sounding siege weapon was the "ballista", which was a giant crossbow that fired massive arrows at defending soldiers. We say cool, but it definitely wasn't cool if you were on the receiving end and became part of a soldier kebab. And NO, you can't take one to the beach to use on sandcastles.

The emptying of the loo into the moat was another form of defence in a way – who wants to swim across THAT? Moats could be as much as 9 metres deep (which is about the length of six 10-year-olds standing on top of each other), so the only way across was a drawbridge, which could be lifted up when the castle was under attack. They could be filled with smelly water or sharpened sticks if they were dry, so for attackers it was a choice between stinky drowning or being pronged to death. Or running away (we choose that option).

Which sounds like an EXCELLENT point to stop talking about this and move on.

KNIGHTS AND TOURNAMENTS

It's school sports day and you're out for REVENGE.

Last year Gary Rimbleton just beat you to the glory of first place in the egg and spoon race, but this year? This year you're **BACK** – and you won't settle for second.

You set off, eyes fixed on the finishing line, your fist gripping that spoon like your life depends on it. Soon you're hurtling along. Not a wobble. You're on **FIRE!**

And just as you reach the line, with victory surely yours, you trip on a lollipop stick. Your egg flies into the air, then lands on your head with a sharp "crack" as you fall to the ground in utter shame and despair.

But if you think *YOU'VE* **GOT IT BAD**, at his sports day, King Henry II of France **DIED** when a lance pierced his visor. Which is quite a bit worse than dropping an egg on your noggin.

Ouch, I think I have something in my eye.

Errr, just a bit.

OK, it wasn't a school sports day, it was a jousting tournament, but it's the same thing (sort of).

If you lived in a medieval castle, you'd have been no stranger to jousting – or to the guys who did it. We're talking **KNIGHTS!**

Your dad might have been a knight, and you could have even worked for one if you were a boy over the age of seven.

First up, what exactly was a knight?

Knights were in charge of the soldiers in a castle. Their job was to make sure the castle and the lord's and lady's family were protected from enemy armies. They could also be expected to go off and fight in wars for the king or on behalf of the church.

Most churches nowadays just expect you to help with bake sales or be nice to your neighbour, which is **FAR** less messy and painful than going to war.

Knights were very important members of the castle and usually came from wealthy or noble backgrounds. If successful, they could become **FAMOUS** and **MEGA-RICH**. They'd earn titles and land and could even end up building a castle of their own.

I'm so famous I should have my own TV show!

What's TV?

But if you were a poor kid, you could more or less **FORGET** any dreams of becoming a knight. Armour and weapons were very expensive, so if you were the child of a servant or peasant there was only one way you could afford to become a knight. You'd need to be spotted at the castle using weapons or being **AMAZING** at fighting and then the lord might help pay for your training.

KNIGHTS AND TOURNAMENTS

For those boys who did get to become knights, their role could begin as early as the age of seven (and it was just boys, which as usual seems extremely unfair on girls who fancied some armoured adventure)!

> Errr, n-n-no. Carry on. Good girl.

> You got a problem with me practising my skills with this EXTREMELY sharp lance?

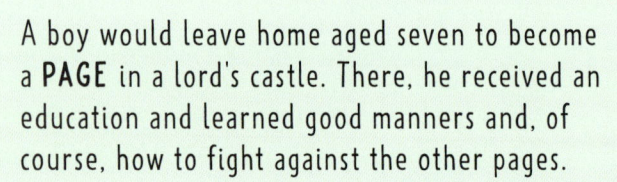

A boy would leave home aged seven to become a **PAGE** in a lord's castle. There, he received an education and learned good manners and, of course, how to fight against the other pages.

When he was 14, he'd become a **SQUIRE** to an actual knight. He had **LOTS** of jobs to do, like cleaning his master's armour and helping him get ready for battle. He'd train with weapons like swords, shields and lances, and learn to ride **HUGE** war horses.

Squires even went into battle alongside their knights sometimes. So if your dad ever asks if you'd like to go to work with him one day, just check to see if he's wearing a metal suit and carrying a sword before you say yes.

> Any chance you could get a job in an office instead?

By the age of 21, a squire could become a full knight and generally go about the place getting all **KNIGHTY** up in people's faces with their knight pals.

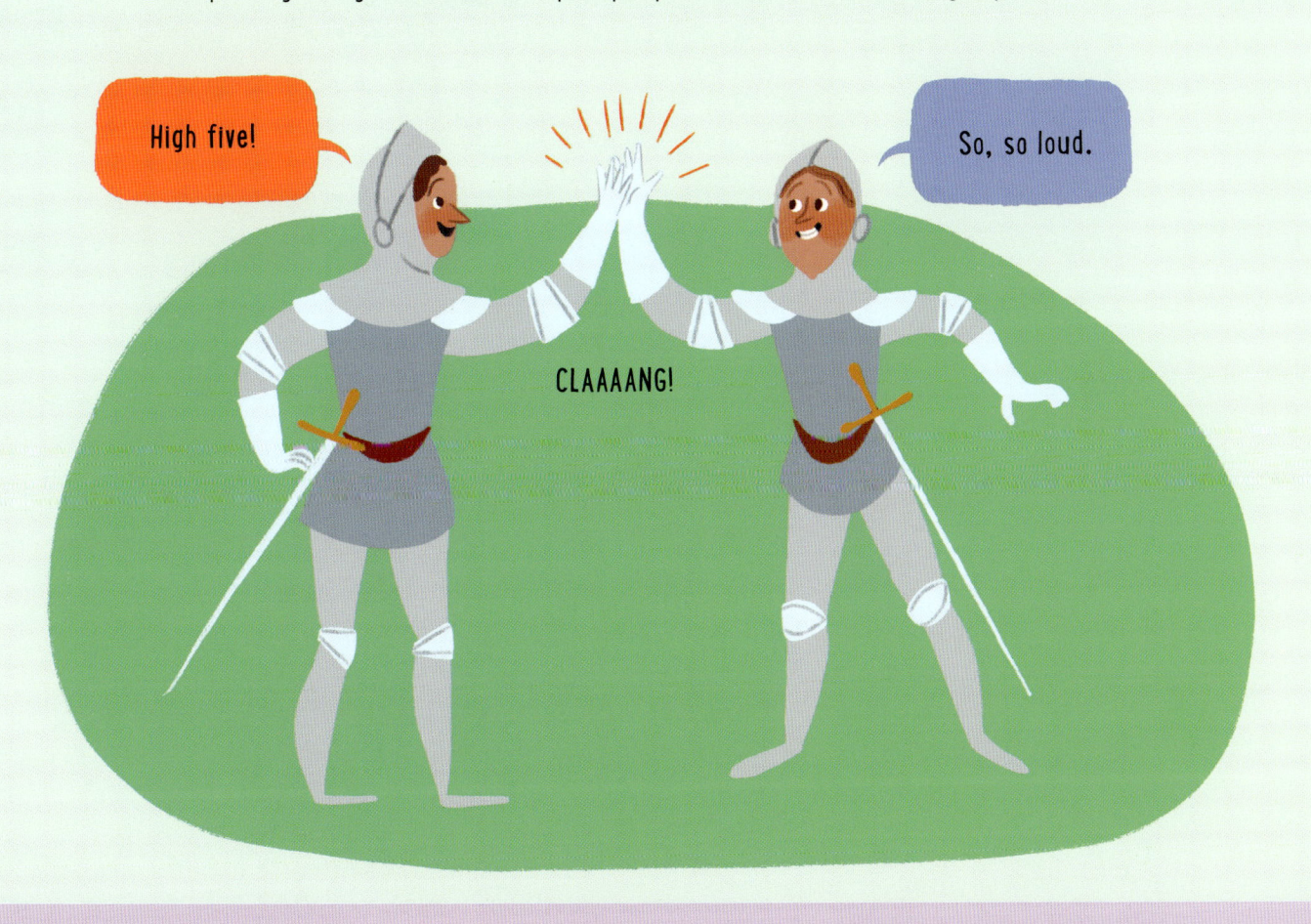

> High five!

> So, so loud.

CLAAAANG!

KNIGHTS AND TOURNAMENTS

Do you ever wish . . . your pals thought you were a total LEGEND?

Maybe they do – but are you actually a legend? We're talking King Arthur style.

People in medieval castles **LOVED** a good story, and there were few as exciting and epic as the tales of Arthur and his Knights of the Round Table.

Whether or not King A was a real guy or a completely made-up character still causes big arguments to this day. There's very little evidence for his existence, but that didn't stop medieval storytellers really going for it. He was said to have been made king after pulling a magic sword called **EXCALIBUR** out of a stone. There was also a sorcerer called Merlin on the scene and one of Arthur's knights, Lancelot, was the child of a fairy queen. If your mum is 10 centimetres tall, has wings and a pretty little crown, you might be, too.

In one tale, Arthur and his knights are having a feast when a green giant on a huge green horse bursts in carrying a holly branch in one hand and an axe in the other. And he didn't even have an invitation! Rude.

Other popular legends from the time include the well-known tale of Robin Hood and the story of Saint George and the Dragon.

So if **YOU** want to be considered a legend, you're going to have to get yourself a sword, a bow and arrows and some armour. Oh, and a dragon, too.

When they weren't hitting enemies with sharp things, knights had to keep training like mad to make sure their skills were always tip-top. Part of that training was taking part in tournaments.

Tournaments – or "tourneys" as they were also known – were basically a huge load of guys in armour pretending to have battles. They were incredibly popular forms of entertainment as well as **VITAL** training.

Knights would travel from far and wide to take part in tournaments – even to different countries. One that took place at Lagny-sur-Marne in France in 1179 was attended by **3,000 KNIGHTS** who'd come from all over the country, as well as from England, Scotland, Germany and Spain.

It was too far to walk all that way, so presumably they took the knight-bus.

Tournaments were a little on the rough side. Sometimes there would be two "armies" mock-fighting against each other, with one group charging the other on horseback to try to **SMASH** through them. These battles were called "melees".

> Ow! You poked me with your spear!

> You started it! You trampled me with your horse!

One of the most popular events was jousting, during which two knights faced each other on horseback, wearing full armour and holding long wooden lances. They'd charge towards each other at **FULL SPEED** before lowering their lances and aiming right at their opponent.

The aim was to either knock the other knight off his horse or smash their lance against his shield or helmet.

Have you ever thought about taking up table tennis instead?

FANCY THAT!

The winner of a jousting match at a tournament got to keep the loser's horse and armour, which were very valuable. He could then charge a lot of money to return them. Asking to keep everyone else's trainers if you win the sack race at your village fair might not go down too well.

If this sounds a little bit on the **"DON'T DO THAT, YOU IDIOTS!"** side of dangerous, you're right.

If you've ever had a splinter in your finger, you'll know it really hurts. So imagine how much a massive shard of wood from a shattered lance would sting if it went right through your head. You'd **DEFINITELY** need a plaster.

Serious injuries and death were not uncommon at tournaments, which suggests they were probably a little more on the risky side than your school sports day.

If that isn't the case, the egg and spoon situation must have got **REALLY** out of hand!

FUN AND GAMES

It's one of those days. You are SO bored. You've played all your games, all your friends are out of town, there's nothing on TV or the ENTIRE internet, you've picked your nose until you've actually scraped your brain and you've counted every single piece of fluff on your carpet (3,795 to be exact).

There's literally **NOTHING** to do. You're even considering starting a conversation with your parents about how your day at school was.

OK, you're not **THAT** bored.

But if you think *YOU'VE GOT IT BAD*, at least your choice of entertainment doesn't include a man doing bottom burps while jumping and whistling.

We know, we know, that actually sounds pretty funny. But if you consider the kind of things he might have had to eat in medieval times (see the chapter on diet if you enjoy feeling queasy) you really have to think again. It might have sounded hilarious, but it wouldn't have **SMELLED** hilarious.

What do you think of his act?

It stinks. Literally!

The man in question was called "Roland the Farter" (or Roulandus le Fartere, as he was also known). He lived in England in the 12th century and his job was to entertain King Henry II, an **IMPORTANT CHAP** who was no stranger to castles.

He did that by capering around as a jester and performing his speciality, which was referred to as "unum saltum et siffletum et unum bumbulum". That translates as "one jump, one whistle and one bottom burp".

It might sound like a pretty limited stage act, but it must have been an absolutely **EPIC** trouser trumpet because he was given a big house called Hemingstone Manor in Suffolk and 30 acres of land in return for his services. Get eating those beans and cabbages now – you could make a **FORTUNE**!

Do you ever wish . . . you were the funniest person in your whole school and everyone thought you were HILARIOUS?

Try putting on a brightly coloured costume, including a hat with bells and donkey ears, and tumbling around poking fun at the headteacher to her face. If it doesn't get you expelled for **LIFE**, it might earn you the title of the best jester in the land.

Jesters were popular entertainers in medieval castles, often employed full-time by a king or lord. Also known as "fools", they capered around, being generally silly and telling jokes. Think a combination of a clown and a comedian and you're there.

As well as wearing his garish outfit and distinctive cap, he might also have an inflated pig's bladder on a stick. So if you see a pig going around looking **VERY** annoyed, a jester might have stolen its bladder. Poor pig.

The jester's jokes could be really rude and they could get away with mocking their master, other lords or even kings. They might have looked silly, but they had to be pretty sharp-witted, so they knew how far to go without getting the chop for being cheeky! Which is probably worth bearing in mind before you take the mickey out of the headteacher.

FUN AND GAMES

Thankfully, jesters making rude jokes weren't the only source of fun in the castle.

Knights in armour on horses were popular toys. As a kid in a castle you would have seen plenty of the real deal going about – your dad might even have been a knight – so having toy versions makes sense.

Other toys that have been discovered by archaeologists include tiny pots and pans, spinning tops and dolls, while board games like chess and backgammon were also popular.

If you're considering burying your brother's beloved games console so that future archaeologists can dig it up in a **FEW HUNDRED YEARS**, please ask your parents first. Hint: they'll say no.

Ball games were all the rage too, but there were no sports shops to nip into to buy your precision-engineered, scientifically balanced, superstar-endorsed ball. No, things were a bit more basic back then.

If you were lucky, you'd get a ball made from leather stuffed with horsehair. Slightly less pleasant-sounding is a ball made from a **PIG'S BLADDER** filled with dried peas.

Next time you go for a kick-about in the playground just imagine scoring a goal with a pea-filled bladder. Although it's definitely better than scoring a goal with a pee-filled bladder.

Why does that angry pig keep staring at us?

Umm, I think we have something that belongs to him.

One ball game that was popular at the time of the great castles was "camping" or "campball", which you might have gone to watch. Despite the name, it had nothing to do with tents – it was more like rugby, although it seems to have been less about how good you were at passing and scoring and more about how good you were at kicking and punching!

At the end of every match there would be plenty of black eyes, bloody noses and broken bones, and serious injuries weren't uncommon. Sometimes people even **DIED** playing it. Presumably you'd get a red card for killing an opposing player, because it's **REALLY** unsporting.

> And the score at the end of that match is 27 broken limbs, to 19.

FANCY THAT!

A report from 1280 of a ball game in Northumberland, England, states that a player was killed after running against an opposing player's dagger! That would definitely be a free-kick, or even a penalty, surely. Red card? Yes . . . because it was covered in blood!

Another form of entertainment, particularly for rich kids, was shooting with bows and arrows, either at targets or while hunting. King Edward I's son, Henry, had two arrows bought for his use in 1274 at the age of **FIVE**, which would probably be frowned on these days. Very sharp sticks and five-year-olds don't really mix.

Poorer children in the castle wouldn't have been able to afford expensive games and toys, but they could make rag dolls, called "poppets", and there were plenty of free games that were as popular then as they are now, like hide-and-seek, **TUG OF WAR** and tag.

People loved going to fairs and markets, where there was plenty to see and do. You might have watched jugglers throwing blazing firesticks up in the air alongside acrobats and musicians. There might also have been dancing bears and tumbling monkeys on show. Definitely **NOT** the kind of thing you're going to see (or want to see) at your local theme park these days.

And when it was winter and the castle grounds and the land outside was covered in snow, everyone – rich or poor – could enjoy building snowmen and having snowball fights.

One word of advice, though. Knocking the king or queen's crown off with a snowball is probably not a good idea if you're allergic to dungeons.

So there you have it. Bottom burps, bladders and brutal ballgames. Sounds like modern boredom is a **LOT** safer than medieval mayhem!

FUN AND GAMES

STILL THINK YOU'VE GOT IT BAD?

Look where we are - it's the end of the book!

Have you enjoyed your journey through castle life?
Did you have fabulous fun reading about all those **HORRIBLE** things?

There, there, no need to cry. We know you **LOVED** this book, so please do feel free to start again and give it another read. It'll be good for your lovely brain.

Of course, if you had lived in a medieval castle you wouldn't have had time to do all this reading. You'd have been **FAR** too busy filling buckets **FULL OF POOP**, eating dolphins and learning loads of Latin off by heart.

> There must be better ways to earn pocket money.

> Stop talking and keep filling that bucket.

And if that doesn't remind you how good you have it today, let's just refresh your memory, **SHALL WE?**

Entertainment today: Games consoles/TV/internet.
Entertainment then: A man doing bottom burps while whistling/kicking a **PIG'S BLADDER** around.

Food today: Pasta/pizza/cheeseburgers.
Food then: Pig's head/peacock/otter.

> Wilhelmina, you haven't eaten all of your pig's head!

> Sorry – I had too much peacock to start and I'm full up.

> Well at least finish your otter.

STILL THINK YOU'VE GOT IT BAD?

Chores now: Tidy room/vacuum/empty dishwasher.
Chores then: Help clean toilet pit/sweep horse manure from stables/turn meat over a fire for **HOURS**.

What do you think? It seems like an open and shut case to us. Life now is pretty **PEACHY** compared with the kind of things kids experienced back then.

Having said that, if you adore the idea of people using a massive catapult to hurl dead bodies and poo over your garden walls, perhaps you **WOULD** be better off back then.

Don't forget to ask for that time machine for your next birthday . . .

61

GLOSSARY

From feasts and jousting to **MURDER HOLES**, it's been quite a ride. Your cranium must be crying out after being **CRAMMED** with all the fabulous facts you've just read! Well, strictly speaking, most of it was fact – some things were just for giggles.

If you want to know **EVEN MORE** about medieval times, here's some bonus interesting stuff to squeeze into your noggin.

ASTRONOMY
This is the scientific study of the universe and all of the stuff that's in it, from the moon and the sun to planets, stars and galaxies. Studying the UNIVERSE is a pretty big subject, so you'll probably need more than one jotter to take notes in.

BACKGAMMON
Backgammon is a board game played with dice in which players try to move their circular counters into one corner and then off the board altogether. It's one of the oldest games in existence – possibly up to 5,000 years old. Despite the name, it has nothing to do with pig-related food and should not be confused with frontbacon or sidesausage.

BOTTLE DUNGEON
This is a place where naughty bottles were kept to teach them a lesson. Or was it? No, it wasn't – it was a basement room which you could only get in or out of via a hatch or hole in a high ceiling. Most often they were actually castle storerooms but could also be used for holding prisoners.

GATEHOUSE
The gatehouse was right at the front of the castle and was where the doors were located. It was the part most vulnerable to attack, so it had the heaviest defences, obstacles and traps to snare intruders. Think of it like your front porch, but with more bows and arrows.

GRIFFIN
The griffin is a legendary creature with the body, tail, and back legs of a lion; the head and wings of an eagle and an eagle's talons as its front feet. As mythical beasts go, it was one of the most impressive, and you'd probably get a funny look or two if you took your pet griffin for a walk in your local park.

LANCE
The lance is basically a big stick. Well, sort of. It's a relative of the spear – like a spear's much bigger, heavier uncle. Unlike the spear, it was meant for carrying rather than throwing. Mounted knights could charge with their lances or they could be used as defence. Jousting lances could measure 3.7 metres or more, so you can forget taking one to class in your schoolbag.

LATIN
Latin was the language of ancient Rome and its empire, which covered lots of Europe, Asia and North Africa at its height. Even after the end of the empire, it was used as the main language of religion and education, and people still study and learn it today. Try telling your parents you're learning it, so if they want you to do a chore, they have to ask you in Latin.

MONK
Medieval monks were men who chose to live a very religious existence by giving up their everyday lives and all their possessions. They'd live in monasteries with other monks and spend their time praying, worshipping and working. And why did monastery doors always smell of bananas? Because they were opened with monk-keys of course!

NOBLE

A nobleman or noblewoman was a person of the highest social group. They were the lords and ladies, the barons and baronesses. Basically, they were the super-posh folk who ruled the land and owned all the castles. If they'd had aeroplanes back then, they could have travelled round the world and become global-nobles. But they didn't.

PEASANT

A peasant was someone who owned or rented a small piece of land for growing crops or keeping animals on. They were basically the opposite of a noble, in that they had little money and no power. The life of a peasant could be tough. Not to be confused with pheasants, which are birds that don't own small pieces of land to keep animals on. That would just be weird.

PHASES OF THE MOON

When you see the moon looking big and round, then smaller and smaller until there is no moon, that isn't because it's running low on batteries – it's going through its phases. There are eight phases (or shapes): new, waxing crescent, first quarter, waxing gibbous, full moon, waning gibbous, third quarter, waning crescent. Gibbous is our new favourite word (it means bigger than a semi-circle but less than a circle).

PHILOSOPHER

A philosopher is someone who studies, thinks and writes about the meaning of life. Plato and Socrates were very famous Greek philosophers. Plato thought about the meaning of plates and Socrates thought about the meaning of socks. (Please don't tell your teacher that or else she'll think you're a nincompoop!)

PORTCULLIS

Portcullises were heavy latticed gates that could be lowered in the blink of an eye to protect the castle doors in the event of an attack. They were made of iron or wood and slid down vertical grooves in the walls of the castle, lowered on ropes or chains. If your bro or sis is always snooping around your stuff, consider installing a portcullis over your bedroom door.

ROBIN HOOD

Robin Hood was a legendary hero from English folklore. According to the story, he was an outlaw and an expert archer and swordsman. He was said to rob from the rich and give to the poor and had a gang of fellow outlaws to help him. Just to be clear, don't rob from anyone – especially not with a bow and arrow. Saying "Well, Robin Hood did it!" will not cut the mustard with the police.

SERF

A serf was even poorer and less powerful than a peasant. Serfs were little more than enslaved people under the total control of their master, the lord of the castle. They worked the land for no pay and could even be bought and sold. So if someone asks if you want to go surfing, just check they didn't actually mean serfing, as it's much less fun.

STONEMASON

In medieval times, stonemasons were very highly thought of and were essential to castle building. They cut, prepared and built with stone, but they also had the skills of an architect, designer and engineer. Without stonemasons, castles would have been built from wood, feathers or jelly, which is frankly useless.

WAR HORSE

Knights needed horses to carry them into war, and they couldn't be shy and retiring. They had to be huge, strong, fierce beasts, and the best were very expensive. Stallions were often used due to their natural aggression – they were described as "biting and kicking" on the battlefield and were even seen fighting each other! We'll stick to cute little Shetland ponies, thanks very much.

INDEX

Animals 6, 8-9, 10, 11, 15, 16-17, 21, 24-25, 26, 32-33, 36, 41, 43, 45, 48, 50, 55, 57, 58-59, 61
Archaeologists 43, 58
Armour 17, 13, 16-17, 25, 44, 46-47, 48, 50-51, 52-53, 54-55, 58
Arrows 11, 44, 46, 48-49, 53, 59
Ballista 49
Bathing 10-11, 15
Battles 16-17, 44-45, 46-47, 48-49
Bloodletting 40-41
Braies 18
Beds 8, 10
Bottle dungeon 31
Candles 9, 23, 30, 36
Campball 58
Castles 6-7, 8-9, 10-11, 15, 21, 23, 34, 36, 44-45, 46-47, 48-49
Catapults 45, 47, 49, 61
Chores 22-23, 24-25, 61
Clothes 16-17, 18-19
Coat of arms 17
Crumhorn 35
Diet 8-9, 13, 23, 24, 25, 32-33, 34-35, 36-37, 39, 45, 61
Disease 41-42
Dogs 6, 8, 15, 12, 24, 45
Doublet 18
Education 23, 24-25, 26-27, 28-29, 30-31, 43, 52, 60
Escoffion 20
Farming 13, 21, 24, 30
Games 25, 56-57, 58-59
Gatehouse 44, 46, 48
Gong farmer 22
Gorget 18
Great Hall 8
Griffin 17
Hair 20-21
Herbs 10, 25, 39, 41, 43

Horses 7, 16, 21, 24, 45, 48, 50, 52, 53, 55, 58, 61
Houppelande 24
Hurdy-gurdy see Crumhorn
Hygiene 7, 8, 10-11, 15, 22-23, 24, 36-37, 39, 49
Illness 38-39, 40-41, 42-43, 50, 59
Jester 56-57, 58, 60
Jewellery 19
Jousting 50, 55
Kirtle 18
Knights 13, 16-17, 25, 43, 46-47, 50-51, 52-53, 54-55, 58
Lance 16, 50, 52, 55
Latin 26, 28, 60
Leeches 40-41
Legends see Myths and Legends
Lizard 35
Lute 29, 35
Naming 14
Noble 6, 12-13, 23, 37, 51
Mangonel 49
Marriage 12
Medicine 25, 38, 40-41, 42-43
Melee 54
Moat 6-7, 11, 22, 48-49
Monks 21
Monsters 15
Music 28-29, 35, 59
Myths and Legends 15, 17, 53
Pattens 19
Peasants 13, 24-25, 29, 51
Philosophers 34
Plague 42
Poor 11, 12-13, 18-19, 20, 24, 28, 30, 34-35, 45, 51, 59
Poppets 59
Portcullis 11, 48
Punishment 30-31
Religion 41

Robin Hood 53
Roland the Farter 57
Rich 11, 12-13, 17, 18-19, 26, 28, 32-33, 34, 47, 51, 59
School 13, 26-27, 28-29, 30-31
Serfs 13
Servants 6, 8, 23, 51
Sieges 44-45, 46-47, 48-49
Siege towers 46
Shields 17, 52, 55
Soldiers 11, 43, 46, 48-49, 51
Smallpox 42
Stonemason 11
Subtleties 34
Swords 13, 16, 25, 43, 46, 48, 51, 52-53
Tanner 23
Teeth 15, 37, 38-39, 40
Toilet 7, 15, 22, 48-49, 61
Tournament 50-51, 54-55
Toys 58-59
Trebuchet 49
Trencher 35
Truckle/trundle 10
Weapons 16, 44, 46-47, 49, 51, 52-53, 54-55
Werewolf 15
Wimple 20
Work 11, 12-13, 18, 22-23, 24-25, 30, 51, 52
Writing 26-27